I0035580

Student Loan Exit Plan

By

Laurick Ingram

The best time to have a Student Loan Exit Plan is when you decide to take out the loan. The second-best time is now.

–Laurick Ingram, Founder
Student Loan Exit Plan

Table of Contents

Foreword

Imagine it's your college graduation day. Your friends and family are in the audience. You're so happy you are almost levitating above your seat. This was not high school, where someone woke you every day and made sure you did your homework. This was college, where you woke yourself up and decided to complete your assignments. Every day was not pretty, all classes weren't fun, but you did it.

Or you decided later in life, you wanted more and went back to school as an adult. With all the adult responsibilities—maybe a spouse, a child, an elderly parent—you still got your butt back in school. Now it is graduation day. You've finished.

Now, imagine you are debt free. Even if you're not, you can imagine you are and remember Einstein said, "Imagination is more important than fact."

A lot of today's student loan debt in fact comes from a lack of or the wrong type of imagining. Many debtors imagine themselves hopelessly in debt, while others imagine they can defer payments indefinitely, and others imagine somehow their debt will be magically forgiven. The result of these imaginings is burgeoning debt, decreasing net worth, and the emergence of the working-class poor.

How the Student Loan Exit Plan was Born.

I was in Broward County, Florida, giving a presentation, on personal money management, explaining the powerful effect of your mindset about money. I was explaining how giving and saving as little as a dollar-a-day could change your financial future. Michelle, a medical school student, raised hand and when I called her said, "But I have $240,000 in student loan debt." Fiddlesticks me, I thought—actually that's not the word I thought, but in case kids are is reading this, that's the word I will go with. I did not know what she *should* do, but that statement lit a fire in me to learn what someone in her situation *could* do.

From there, I learned about half the people I was speaking to had student loan debt ranging from $6,500 to her staggering $240,000. Yikes! For them my dollar-a-day message sounded like someone giving a person dying of thirst an eye-dropper full of water and saying it's going to be okay.

Michelle's question was the flashpoint that launched me on a quest to understand the breadth and scope of student loan debt in America. After speaking with hundreds of families who either did or did not use student loans to finance their educations, I arrived at two conclusions. First, a student loan is a mortgage on the student's future and should only be used with proper advice and a payoff plan. Second, whether you are managing a dollar-a-day or a thousand-dollars-a-day, your mindset towards money can make you or break you. Consequently, the Student Loan Exit Plan was founded with a focus on guiding people with student loans from loaning their futures to owning their futures. My heart's desire is that the ideas in this book will prosper you, not harm you; give you hope and a future.

What is the Student Loan Exit Plan?

The Student Loan Exit Pan is a multi-step approach for people who are either heading to college and plan to take out loans; are in college and already have loans; or have graduated or dropped out of college and have to repay loans.

The plan provides online or in person; one-on-one or group coaching that covers:

- Loan Disclosures Explained

- Real Time, Real Money Payback Plans

- Borrower / Lender Collaboration

- Parent—Faculty—Student—Lender Cohorts

- Partnerships with Other Organizations

- Accountability Partners

You can learn more about us at https://giveandsave365.com.

Author's Note: I could not have written this book without the transparency of the people I interviewed who shared what they did right and what they did wrong in their college and financial lives. All the stories shared are true; however, no real names are used. This is because I promised confidentiality to anyone who agreed to be interviewed. Moreover, the intent behind sharing these personal stories is not to embarrass but empower people with student loans. Anyone who chose to identify themselves and share their stories could do so on my social media platforms, blogs, and podcasts.

Congratulations!

Congratulations! If you are reading this book, it means you value learning. Either you or someone your care about is on the way to college, already in college, or graduated from a college—and by college, I mean college, university, or any other post-secondary education. I am proud of you and hope you are proud of yourself. Anything worth having is worth working for and paying for and this book is about helping you pay for your education using the smartest ways possible. Because learning is what you want, we want to help you on that wonderful journey. We are so proud of you! If you want to go to school, we want to help you get there; if you are in school, we want you to finish; if you have already graduated, we want to make sure you get the most out of your economic future. It means you know there is value in education, and you want more of it.

If you are in college or headed to college or some other school, or if someone you support is in college or headed to college, do you have the money to pay for that school? Or will you have to take out loans, rely on grants, scholarships, work study, your family, or some combination of the above? If you are already attending college or have graduated, chances are you are among the one-in-five Americans who have student loan debt. If any of these facts apply to you or someone you know, grab hold of the ideas in this book and don't let go.

I am all for post-secondary education, I graduated Miami-Dade College, my wife graduated from Eastern Illinois University, and our sons graduated from the University of Florida and Florida International University. At the time of this writing, our oldest son just completed his master's degree at Teachers College, Columbia University's Graduate School of Education. My wife and I both took out student loans to get through undergraduate school, but our sons finished undergrad with scholarships, work study, and help from their mother and me. Many of our sons' friends; however, took out loans to finance their education. My son Josh tells me that right now student loans are a "volatile" issue. He explained that college cost of attendance has inflated in addition to cost of living and education requirements for jobs, but American wages have remained stagnant for decades. This means it's almost a requirement to have some sort of post-secondary education but it's nowhere near as affordable as it was in the past. People are essentially paying more for less."

Although, there is a lot of evidence to support those assertion, this is not a campaign for nor against the student loan process in its current form. This is a plan to teach you how to know what you owe and get started paying your loans back as quickly as you can (like today), so that you will eventually owe nothing.

Two challenges you will face are (1) getting above the noise of life (for example, if you are reading or listening to this on your phone, you are probably checking your social media feeds—aha caught you!—as well); and (2) procrastination. Whether you're in school or not, everyday you're flooded with information from your phone, your tablets, the television, the radio, and on and on. Whether you know it or not, a lot of that information is designed to move money away from you: buy this plan, buy that music, buy this shirt, buy these tickets, buy, buy, buy, buy. Before you know it, you're saying bye-bye to your money.

What you buy and how much you buy is up to you, but the smart thing to do is make sure some of the money that comes your way moves you forward financially. For that to occur, you must decide you want it to happen, then do something to make sure it happens automatically. The automation is a critical step in the process because once something becomes automatic, you do not have to keep repeating the decision-making process.

The first week I started working, I set up an automatic deduction to come from my pay and deposit into my savings account. Every time I got paid, the amount automatically transferred, which means every two weeks, I did not have to re-decide to do it, it was done. A core belief of the Student Loan Exit Plan is that small things done are better than great things planned. Here is proof: if you take out a non-subsidized student loan for $10,000 and make no payments for the next four years at an interest rate of 4%, interest is accumulating at a little over a dollar a day. In four years, when you are ready to pay it back, the amount is now $11,732. That small accumulation of a dollar a day in interest has increased your loan amount 17% before you make your first payment.

To write this book, I interviewed hundreds of people who went to college or post-secondary schools. Some took out student loans and some did not. The lowest amount borrowed was $6,500 and the greatest amount was $250,000. Using that dollar-a- day yardstick, imagine how much interest is owned on those loans.

Enough about the challenges. this book focuses on a solution of making small things work for you instead of against you. This book is not a technical guide written in the language of a software development disclosure. It is written in plain language to address the decision-making process that leads to families borrowing money for college; then the process and plan they use to pay it back.

Let's get started.

Action Step

- Finish reading this book and apply what you learn.

Breakfast with Einstein

I was having breakfast at one of my favorite soul food restaurants, when I could not figure out why whenever I sat down that day, my jeans would slide downward exposing the elastic band on my underwear. Betty is my regular waitress who is full of attitude and quick to serve up unsolicited advice. She told me, "Your underwear is showing." As I stood to hitch up my jeans for the umpteenth time that day, Betty said, "It's because you missed two belt loops in the back." Soon as I slipped my belt through the loops, the problem was solved.

After I finished my chicken and waffles, I left Betty a big tip and thanked her for advice. She smiled a crooked smile and said, "You can't fix a problem doing the same thing that caused the problem. You put your belt on wrong and pulling your pants up all day was not going to change that." I asked her if she ever read Einstein, and she gave me dead eyes, and asked, "Are you trying to be funny?"

I was not trying to be funny, but Einstein said, "We can't solve problems by using the same kind of thinking we used when we created them," which is exactly what I was trying to do. Betty said, "Whatever, see you next Sunday." Like I said full of attitude and my favorite waitress. I said, "Have a good one Betty!"

What do Betty and Einstein have to do with student loans? Before I explain that, here is some background on student loans in America. The percentage of students who take loans in America is staggering. What is even more alarming is the percentage of those with student loan debts. If you walk into any post-secondary institution, chances are one out of every ten students you come across has student loan debt. In 2019, NBC news reported that one in five adult Americans has debts from student loans. If these statistics are not bad enough, as years go by, college tuition prices keep increasing. The inference is that student loan debt will continue increasing. As the loans keep increasing, so does the burden on students to pay them off. It is a never-ending cycle.

In 2019, Forbes magazine reported student loan debt was reported to be the second-highest source of consumer debt in the U.S. This means that it was ahead of debts due to credit cards and auto loans, but second only to home mortgages.

This situation cuts across all age groups and demographics. A 2018 study conducted by the Federal Reserve Bank of New York found that more than 44.7 million Americans have student loan debts. Although it is safe to say that the bulk of these Americans are young people, NBC News reports that there is another age group whose percentage is just as high as that of the young people; they are adults aged 60 and above. How could this be? For some, it is the debts of their student loans that they have yet to pay off. For others, it is the debts they had to take on for either their children or grandchildren. These reasons and more are why there is a student loan debt accruing to about $1.5 trillion in America in 2019.

It is impossible to impact a debt this size without unpacking the thinking that created it. One of the key factors is the borrower seeing the debt in abstract terms—something out there they will deal with later, rather than the in the concrete terms the lender uses to account for every dollar of interest that accumulates daily.

Whatever levels of thinking created this

14

situation, a radically different type of thinking will

be required to fix it. Take some tips from Betty or

Einstein, check your belt loops, pull up your pants,

and create new levels of thinking for yourself.

Action Steps

- For the next seven days, spend at least five minutes a day thinking about what you will do when your life is student loan-free.

A Mortgage on Your Future

A mortgage is a legal agreement by which a bank or other creditor lends money and charges interest on that money in exchange for taking title of the debtor's property, with the condition that the conveyance of title becomes void upon the payment of the debt. In the case of student loans, the debtor's "property" is his or her future earnings. A student loan is essentially a mortgage on the debtor's future. The debt continues whether you are earning money to pay for it or not. If you have earnings, a percentage of the earnings belong to the lender. So much so that if you do not pay those earnings can be garnished. If you file income taxes, in some instances your tax refunds can be seized.

Finally, if you took out a federal student loan and are in default, a portion of your social security benefits can be seized. One of my interviewees was blindsided by this when she was preparing to retire. Essentially, a portion of your social security payments can be garnished if you default on federal student loans. It is called an offset, and more people than ever are losing out on Social Security benefits due to federal student loan debt. In some instances, the government can take up to 15% of the outstanding debt, after allowing for the first $750 of

18

monthly benefits. (For example, if a retiree receives $850 per month in benefits, 15% of that would be $127.50. But since he can't be given less than $750, the most that can be garnished is $100.) This rule applies only to federal student loans, not private loans.

Action Step

- Start making payments today. This way you will buying back your future today rather than waiting for it to be taken from you tomorrow.

Verbal Assets

Robert Kiyosaki, author of *Rich Dad Poor Dad,* wrote: "It doesn't take money to make money," said rich dad. "It takes words. The difference between those who are rich and those who are poor is their financial vocabulary. And the best news is words are free."

Before going further, two words that have distinctly different meanings, but were used interchangeably during my interviews are "can't" and "won't." During my interviews most of the students considering loans or who were already in debt, said, "I 'can't' work my way through college." The more provable statement is "I won't work my way through college." The German philosopher Arthur Schopenhauer said, "Every man takes the limits of his own field of vision for the limits of the world." They are not one and the same.

Can't is a universal absolute, much like the word always; and to quote my late brother Kelsey, "statements that begin with 'always,' are almost always wrong." To assert that something can't be done, is to imply that no one in similar circumstances has done it. No matter your challenge—too young, too old, too tall, to small, too fat, too skinny, single parent, married with children, unattractive gorgeous, disabled, Olympic class athlete, black, white, LBGTQ, straight as an arrow, recovering alcoholic, failed entrepreneur, startup genius—if someone in similar circumstances has ever done it, it can be done. I know of several people who worked their way through college, including my sister who took seven years to get her bachelor's, because she would stop school, work, save money, pay for her classes, then re-enroll.

An aside here is that my best friend went to college on a full scholarship for basketball. His example is a compelling argument for working your way through college, because his practices and playing schedule were brutal and he was still expected to be a full-time student. He did graduate and is now the head scout for the L.A. Lakers. He once told me that in high school, one of the team's drills was 1,000 layups. If that is not work, I don't know what is.

Back to words as assets. A student loan is a liability. There are many definitions of liabilities, but a practical and easy one to understand is that: an asset will feed you, because an asset is something that continues to pay you, hold, or increase its value. Conversely, a liability is something that continues to cost the borrower.

I knew an interior decoratornamed Ricardo. He owned two adjoining condominiums. One he lived in, while the other he rented out. The one he rented

24

netted him a positive cashflow of $1,500 per month, while the mortgaged unit he lived in cost him around $3,500 per month. The mortgage was an asset for the mortgage company, but a liability for Ricardo. If he closed his decorating business and had no other income, the mortgage would eat up his savings month-by-month. If the mortgage company did nothing else, based on the note he had signed he would keep feeding them for the next 360 payments. His mortgage was their asset. The other condo was his asset, because if he did nothing, but except keep his renters in the other condo, it would keep feeding him.

Another way to explain it is if you bought a rental property and it paid you a net profit of $1,500 a month; how many could you afford? Answer as many as you can get your hands on. However, if you owed on the property and each month cost you

$1,500; how many could you afford? Not many and not long unless you have a wild desire to experience the thrill of bankruptcy.

Where the student loan vocabulary gets murky is when students are told their education is an asset. It is an asset, but it is a non-transferrable (you cannot sell or give it to someone else), intangible (unlike art or real estate) asset. More importantly, if the asset is not properly managed and converted into income, it can and will become a liability.

In closing, I would add beware of some words.

I have already emphasized the importance and power of knowing and using good money words. Conversely, bad money words have power as well. I use the word "broke" to illustrate one of the poor money management habits, but do not use it to describe your financial situation. Just as you can plant seeds of prosperity in your mind, you can plant seeds of poverty. Whichever seed you plant, is going to grow. Words like "broke" and "poor" repel money and opportunities to make money.

Action Step

- Commit to never using words like "broke" or "poor" to describe your finances. Phrases like I am budgeting better, buying smart, growing my savings plant seeds of success in your thoughts.

Is a Degree an Asset?

The short answer is "Yes, but…" Previously, we covered the differences in assets versus liabilities. What we will cover in this chapter are classes of assets and liabilities. In our vocabulary arsenal, "class" is a critical word to understand. In this context, class means a set or category of things having some property or attribute in common and differentiated from others by kind, type, or quality. Broadly speaking there are two classes of debts—secured and unsecured. A home mortgage is usually a loan secured by—you guessed it "a home." Credit cards, unless they are tied to equity lines are traditionally unsecured. So, what type of debt is a student loan?

We will answer that shortly, but first I want to discuss two classes of assets, tangible and intangible. A tangible asset is "tangible" because you can see and touch it. Homes, precious metals, jewelry, cars, works of art, etc. are examples of tangible assets. Examples of intangible assets include copyrights, trademarks, stocks (even though a common stock represents owning a share of a company, you cannot exchange a share of the stock for a brick of the company headquarters). College degrees are both intangible and nontransferable. Nontransferable means your degree is yours and yours only. Conversely, the common stocks traded on the New York Stock Exchange are transferrable—they can be sold or given to someone else and are worth whatever the market price is at the time of sale. After the transfer, the recipient now owns that asset. But you cannot sell nor give your degree to someone else, it is yours and yours alone. It is an intangible, nontransferable asset that allows you to apply for many jobs that people without degrees cannot apply for. Until the privilege is converted into a job or profession it has unrealized economic value.

Action Step

- Buy an asset—a piece of art, a stock, a bond, a mutual fund, an exchange traded fund, a certificate of deposit.

Pay Attention

When it comes to student loans the first thing you should pay is attention. Why do I say this? More importantly, what does "Pay Attention" mean? I will answer the second question first. Pay attention means that beyond just reading and signing your loan documents, the key one being the master promissory note (MPN), you must continually know what you are committing to financially. It is continuous because until you pay it off, you are obligated to the terms of the note. Back to why the borrower should pay attention. The borrower should pay attention because the lender paid excruciating attention to detail when they drafted the note, which is why the terms are ironclad. In our chapter on Verbal Assets, we discussed the difference between secured and unsecured liabilities. Most credit cards, not including lines of equity drawn against real estate, are unsecured by an asset. Instead, you are issued the card based on your credit worthiness. If you use the card to charge a vacation, or furniture neither can be repossessed under the terms of the card. A secured loan, such as a car loan is tied to an asset, namely, the car.

"Aha!" you say. Then a student loan is an unsecured loan, because no one can seize my education. True, no one can seize your education, however, depending on which student loan you obtain, it is secured by your pledge that if you fail to pay it back, your wages, your income tax refunds, and (if it is a federally-sponsored loan) possibly a portion of your social security benefits can be seized until the loan, penalties, and interest are paid off.

Most of the people I interviewed (including some with six-figure debt) did not understand these critical terms of their loans. All these conditions are written in the note, but unless the borrower pays attention, they may be missed, until the lender exercises them. After that, the borrower will not only pay attention, but chances are he or she will never forget.

Some of the questions I asked my interviewees were:

What is your loan's interest rate?

Is your loan subsidized or unsubsidized?

How much interest is accumulating daily?

When is your first payment due?

When will you make your last payment?

If you owe more than $5,000 and this was the low end, many graduate students owed more than $50,000, these types of answers indicate the borrower is not paying attention.

Q: What is your loan's interest rate?

A: I am not sure. Or I have more than one loan and different rates, but I don't know what the overall rate is.

Q: Is your loan subsidized or unsubsidized?

A: What does the mean. Or subsidized, I think.

Q: How much interest is accumulating daily?

A: I don't really think of it that way. (Your lender does.)

Q: When is your first payment due?

A: Six months after I graduate, maybe.

Q: When will you make your last payment?

A: Almost no one had a specific date for this one.

Most people finance new cars, which are usually substantial investments. It is difficult to comprehend how students, or their families can borrow large amounts of money with no more than a vague understanding of when and how it will be paid back as well as what will happen if it is not paid back.

Action Step

- Pay attention answering the questions posed in this chapter:

  ➢ What is your loan's interest rate?

  ➢ Is your loan subsidized or unsubsidized?

  ➢ How much interest is accumulating daily?

  ➢ When is your first payment due?

  ➢ When will you make your last payment?

"Who You Wit?"

In the movie *House Party 3*, the late comedian Bernie Mac played Uncle Vester. In one scene he is giving nephew Christopher "Kid" Reid, a pep talk, before Kid goes to meet his future in-laws. Kid is nervous about meeting his fiancé's parents, but Uncle Vester who is accompanying Kid, asks, "Who you wit?!" Kid says: "Uncle Vester!" What Uncle Vester is letting Kid know is that as long as he's "wit" his Uncle Vester, everything will be all right.

As I talked to people with student loans, one question I would ask was, "Do you know anyone who went to college that did not take out a student loan?" Many of them did not. As they answered, Bernie Mac's voice echoed in my mind, "Who you wit?" Here is why: great athletes tend to surround themselves with great athletes; virtuoso musicians know other virtuosos; actresses with actresses; mechanics with mechanics; fashion designers with fashion designers, video gamers with video gamers. By having people around you who perform at their peaks, you are inspired to perform at your peak.

No matter what you want out of life, four things will help you to get or hinder you from getting those things.

- The people you know—Who you "wit?"
- The words you know—your verbal assets

- The decisions you make—what you imagine yourself doing.

- The actions you take—what you actually do.

Before you read another word, ask yourself, are you

- willing to be "wit" new people?

- willing to increase your verbal assets?

- willing to imagine yourself owning your future?

- willing to take the steps necessary to make the previous steps your new reality?

If you want to pay off your student loans, you need to meet people who have paid or are paying off their loans. You need to learn words like amortization schedule, loan satisfaction, APR—annual percentage rate. But meeting those people and learning those words will only get you part-way to the finish line. To get across that line, you must decide you want to do what they did and use what they used. Finally, you must do those three things, because "knowing ain't doing." If you don't believe me, see how many of your friends and family know daily exercise is good for you; then see how many actually exercise daily.

Whether you bought this book or got it as a gift, if your answer to the four questions posed above is "No," then you will probably not get much out of this book. You would be better off either returning it (we will give you a full refund) or giving it to a friend who is willing to give it a shot.

If your answer to the four questions above is "Yes" or even "Maybe," then you have just taken a huge stride towards buying back your future.

Action Step

- Get "wit" some people who are paying off their student loans and ask them how they are doing it. Take care to note the words they used to describe the process.

FOMO

According to www.dictionary.com FOMO (or fear of missing out) is an anxious feeling you get when you feel other people might be having a good time without you. One historical illustration of this was the Beanie Baby craze, when people were travelling far and wide and paying exorbitant prices for little stuffed animals. The crest of that event was in 1998 when Beanie Babies did more than $1.3 billion in sales. I had a passing familiarity with Beanie Babies, but neither bought nor knew anyone who bought the extravagantly priced stuffed animals.

The incidence of FOMO that I am familiar with is Bitcoin. December 2013, CNN reported: "Bitcoin is a new currency that was created in 2009 by an unknown person using the alias Satoshi Nakamoto. Transactions are made with no middlemen—meaning, no banks! Bitcoin can be used to book hotels on Expedia, shop for furniture on Overstock and buy Xbox games; but much of the hype is about getting rich by trading it. The price of bitcoin skyrocketed into the thousands by 2017."

I have been investing in common stocks, mutual funds, and exchange traded funds for more than 20 years. That being said, one of the things I have learned over that time, was knowing where and when to enter an investment and where and when to exit. I was amazed at the number of people with no investment experience who were investing thousands of dollars in Bitcoin. I am not a crypto currency financial analyst; therefore, I offer no opinion on whether Bitcoin is or is not a good investment. What concerned me was that most of the people (they were under 30) investing in Bitcoin had no clear entry / exit strategy. The underlying reason many of these people were investing was FOMO. Either through the media, urban legend, the grapevine, or trusted associates they kept hearing how Bitcoin's price was going up. Then, real or imagined, how others were making gobs of money buying Bitcoin and they did not want to miss out.

When enough people begin following this approach, you get a herd mentality, where people can be influenced by their peers to adopt certain behaviors on a largely emotional, rather than rational basis.

That mentality seems to be in play with student loans as well. More than half of the borrowers I interviewed said, "All the students I know used loans to pay for college." I refute this statement in the chapter titled "Who you wit'?" Nevertheless, that belief is a basis for many students and those supporting the students to take out loans.

How do you know if you are blindly following the herd? Pay attention and ask good questions.

49

For instance, does the statement "All the students I know" mean the same thing as "All students?" It does not. This is another example of confusing limited personal vision of possibilities with the world of unlimited possibilities. If all the students you know took out loans, maybe it is time you meet the ones who did not take out loans.

Action Step

- Meet one person who completed college without a student loan.

Sell or be Sold

For a good part of my life, I described myself as not being good at selling things. What I did not realize is that many of life's transactions are either "sell or be sold." If you are looking for a job, you are selling a prospective employer on the idea that you are the best fit. If you are looking for a sweetheart, you are selling your prospective canoodler that you are the best person to canoodle with.

After decades of being a non-salesman, I have come to accept that if I believe in something, I have the potential to be the world's greatest salesman. Because of that, I have been able to help myself and thousands of others add value to their lives and the lives of others.

Make no mistake, I am selling you on the value and power of the Student Loan Exit Plan. More importantly, if you have a student loan, someone else has already sold you on the value of the Student Loan Entrance Plan.

Selling a good or service you believe will either increase another's enjoyment or lessen their pain is a noble pursuit. Selling someone something that makes you money but has little or no value to the other person is a con. We are not "con" artists, we are "can" artists. We sell you on the notion that you the master of your fate; you are the captain of your soul.

Action Steps

- Sell an idea, a service, or a product today. It doesn't matter how or for how much, but make sure it's something you believe has value for the other person.

It's Not About the Money

I knew a Drug Enforcement Agent named Rick B. back when the cocaine cartels were big in Miami and a kilo of cocaine sold for around $20,000. When he would be setting up deals to buy from dopers, he would have to run the plan by his bosses. He taught me that whenever a boss said, "It's not about the money," you better believe it's about the money. In the case of student loans, some of your most trusted advisors, counselors, family, and friends will tell you, "It's not about the money, it's about your education." Take a lesson from Rick B.

here: it's about the "money." How do I know? Because I already explained that many student loans although unsecured by an asset, like real estate, or a patent, are secured by an ironclad link to your future earnings. Many student loans cannot be discharged by bankruptcy; your wages can be garnished (attached as money due or property belonging to a debtor by garnishment); the lenders can seize income tax returns; and in some cases lenders can even seize a percentage of the debtor's social security benefits. If someone has advised you that a deal like that "Is not about the money," that person is sorely mistaken. I will go one step further and say not only is it about the money, it is about your mindset towards money, which is as important if not more important that the money itself. If you don't believe that, Research the stories of the countless lottery winners, who go broke within five years. Their financial woes were caused by the ways they thought about and handled money, which I cover in the chapter titled Micro Lotteries.

Action Step

- The next time someone tells you it's not about the money, ask yourself, "Is that person asking me to pay them or are they paying me?" If it's the former, grab hold of your wallet and start looking for the exit.

Micro Lotteries

"What would you do if you won the lottery?" I cannot count the number of times I have heard that question asked. In fact, there used to be a reality show that documented the lives of people after they won the lottery. I watched it a few times, and after a while the stories became cliché. There were basically two groups. People who went broke within five years of winning—some as soon as one year—and people who did not. It was evident that the people who held on to their winnings, had good money habits before they ever won the lottery; whereas, the people who lost their money had poor money habits, which they continued using despite having more money. One key reason these people went broke, was that they had poor ideas and beliefs about money. Giving them more money did not change that fact, it just gave them a bigger stage on which to fail. My dear friends, Mo and Suzy Chorney, counseled that you can always spend more money than you make. If that is your habit, then no matter how much money you make you will still go broke, which is why there are people who make six-figure salaries, who, if they lost their jobs, would be homeless in six months.

In this book I illustrate the power of paying $7

a week to your student loans. Another way to pay off your student loans is the Micro Lottery Strategy. A lottery winning is an unexpected windfall of cash. An unexpected windfall can be anywhere from $100 to several million. What is as important as the windfall is what you do with the money you receive.

Here is a real-life example. When Carlton was 21, his father passed away and left him an insurance policy for $20,000. The first thing Carlton did was go out and buy himself a shiny new car. Since he had little credit, the salesman explained he needed to put $4,000 down to buy a $12,000 car. This was a while back and cars were financed at around 10% interest and the maximum period was three years. His payment was $258. He had a new car, but no place to live. His friend Alvin lived with Alvin's aunt. Carlton asked Alvin if he could stay and pay rent for the room. Alvin's aunt agreed and Carlton moved in agreeing to pay $200 per month for rent. Carlton dragged his feet on getting a job, never paid the rent, but drove around in his shiny new car and went on lots of dates. Once it became obvious Carlton had no intention of paying rent to the aunt, Alvin asked him to leave, which he did. Within six months, whatever was left of the $20,000 was gone and there were still 30 payments remaining on the not-so-new car.

Let's unpack Carlton's story. First, kudos to his

father for providing an inheritance for his son, that was a good thing. This was 40 years ago and $20,000 went a long way. Carlton's first poor decision was to use the money to create more debt. He could have bought a used car and at least there would have been no more monthly payments. Next, he had no plan to save any of the money. By not managing his money, his money was managing him. He did not use the car to get a job right away and create new income. To the best of my knowledge he used none of the money to help anyone else, unless you count drinks, dancing, and dinner dates as charity.

If Carlton had bought a used car for $5,000, invested $5,000 in anything making a return of 7%

and, got a job and partied with the rest, he still would have been better off. With no car loan, his income could have gone toward his living. If he was really smart, he would have saved some of the new income to add to the $5,000 he already had saved and kept building it.

Because of Carlton's weak money management skills, it would not have mattered if he inherited $20,000 or $200,000. If he did the same thing: created debt, had no savings plan, did not work and partied like a rock star, he was on the road to the poor house.

From time to time in your life you will win micro lotteries and run into unexpected windfalls— tax returns, gifts, bonuses. Already have it in your mind, that at least 10% will go toward paying off your student loan. If you want to sharpen your fiscal skills further, save 10% for yourself and give 10% to help someone else. If you do it with a hundred dollars, you will do it with $10,000. Strong money habits work well at all levels.

Action Steps

- Develop and write out your Micro Lottery Plan and the next time money comes to you unexpectedly, follow your plan.

Training for the Race

Tomorrow belongs to those who prepare for it today. Lois began running half-marathons in her sixties but began training in her fifties. Initially, she could not run a mile due to weak knees. She hired a trainer and for several months did strength training. As her legs got stronger, she began to walk a mile or two; then run a mile or two; until she worked herself up to half-marathons.

What is important here is that she did not initially think, "I am going to run half-marathons in my sixties," then waited idly by for her sixties to arrive. She took immediate action then followed through until she could run the race she chose.

One of my interviewees for this book was Ivan, who had gotten his bachelor's, was working on his master's, and planned to go to law school after that. Ivan had over $25,000 in student loan debt, which has variable interest rates. When I asked Ivan for his plan to pay back the loan, he said he would worry about it when he finished school. Essentially, there is a marathon of loan payments in his future, but he expects that when the time arrives, he will be ready. Ivan does not understand that "We don't rise to level of our expectations we fall to the level of our preparations." For the last four years, he has done nothing to train himself to pay back his loan. I hope as I am sure he does, that he will land a great job when he finishes school and make enough money to pay off his student loans and have enough left over to support himself; but hope is an energy not a strategy.

If you took out a student loan, and plan to finish your degree in four years, then four years from now your loan payoff marathon is set to begin. It makes sense to start training today, not in four years. If you took out a student loan, you will have to pay it back, so you may as well start paying it back today. The lenders are also running in the same marathon race, but they start training the day you signed the loan.

When my boys were nine and twelve, being

boys, they would want to race each other. I insisted Josh, the elder, take a few paces back from the start line to give his little brother a shot at winning.

Your student loan is lot like that race. You and the lender start at the same place the day you sign the loan. After that, because of interest, you take a few steps back. Four years from now when the starter pistol fires, the loan payoff marathon will begin. The lender's race begins at the starting line, because the amount loaned to you has not changed. If the lender loaned you $10,000 (although $50,900 is the average cost of one year in a private college, we will use $10,000 for ease of understanding), the amount the lender loaned you and it has not changed. The amount you owe the lender, however, grows daily—yes daily. Every day, you take few steps backwards. If the interest rate on the loan is 4%; four years from signing, your race doesn't start at $10,000, it starts at $11,732, because of the accumulated interest.

This matter because (1) if you borrowed $10,000 and paid it back with no interest over 10 years, your payment would be $10,000 / 120 or $83 per month. If you were paying back just the $11,732 over 10 years, your payment would be $97 per month. What you are actually paying back is $11,732 with interested accumulating on the unpaid balance over the life of the loan. This comes out to be $14,253 or $119 per month. This is important enough to illustrate:

Here it is in a table.

Item	$10,000	$10,000	$10,000
Interest	0% Over the Life of the Loan	4% for the First Four Year Only	4% Over the First Four Years, Plus Interest over the Life of the Loan
Payback Period	10 Years (120 Months)	10 Years (120 Months)	10 Years (120 Months)
Monthly Payment	$83	$90	$101
Total Amount Paid Back	$10,000	$11,732	$14,253
Total Interest Paid	$0	$1,732	$4,253
Percentage Increase on Initial Loan	0%	17%	42%

Here it is in a chart.

$10,000, 10--year Student Loan Marathon
Race 3 --Interest Over the Life of the Loan
Race 2 -- Interest After 4 years
Race 1--No Interest

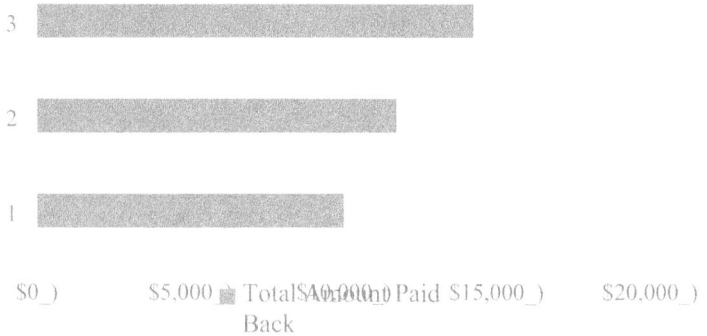

$0_)	$5,000	Total Amount Paid $10,000	$15,000_)	$20,000_)

Back

I wanted to illustrate this in words, as a table, and as a chart because of Shalon, one of my interviewees. I had Shalon read her student loan schedule to me. She had borrowed $25,000 at 7% interest. It did not matter that the paper read that she would be paying back $34,832. She kept repeating, I only owe $25,000. This is another example of the importance of verbal assets and paying attention.

Can you see where this is a hard race for the student borrower to win? This is why you need to begin your training as soon as possible by making payments on that loan the day you get it. If you are paying small amounts, it will not pay off the loan, but what it will do is (1) keep you focused on the balance; (2) train you at how to make you payments; (3) keep you closer to the starting line when your payoff race begins; and (4) (this is a biggie) will give you valuable money management experience, because knowledge accumulates.

Now, in the words of my eleventh-grade math teacher, Lester Sandoval: "Let us move on!"

Action Step

- Start your training today by paying $7.00 on your student loan this week. (If you don't know how to set up the payment or want us to set it up for you, contact us on our website https://giveandsave365.com and we will help.)

Real Money Versus Play Money

I knew a guy named Greg who disarmed bombs for a living. He was fond of saying, "There's a lot to be said for good training, but the best training is experience." This point was driven home for me when I began investing in the stock market. For years, I had a "mock portfolio" of imaginary stocks that I bought and sold. I started out giving myself $1,000,000 to invest. I tried different strategies, to see which ones worked the best. When one did not work, I sold and started again. It was good training to understand, how stocks behaved, what stocks were good performers, test what the financial gurus were betting on, etc. The problem was that I was not gaining real time, real life experience. This was because, to quote investors, "I had no real skin in the game." If the market dropped 100 points, I did not actually lose any money.

After a year or so of managing my "play money" portfolio, I was ready to take the plunge and invest "real money." I transferred $5 million dollars from the trust from left me by my great, great grandfather Uriah, who made his money selling dreams to people who had none. (That was a joke to see if you were paying attention.) Actually, it was $5,000 of my hard-earned savings.

The first remarkable thing that happened was I feared losing my real money. When it was $1,000,000 in play money, I wanted to win, but I was not so afraid of losing. When it was $5,000 of real money, losing it became a central concern. One of the first stocks I bought was $500 worth of RIMM, Research in Motion. RIMM, as I understood it, owned much of the technology that supported the Blackberry. Phones. "What's a Blackberry?" You ask. "Exactly."

I bought it right as Blackberry was being knocked out the box, by smart phones. To date, it has been the largest loss, percentagewise of any stock I bought. The stock went down 62% after I bought it and before I finally sold it. The 62% loss on an investment of $500 equaled a loss of $310. Because—thank God—I had only invested 10% of the $5,000 the loss to my entire portfolio was 6.2% and I still had $4,690 left. Here's the point, when it was play money, the portfolio could drop 6% and be down $60,000, and I would calmly evaluate my next steps. However, once it was my real money that I worked for, losing $310 was jarring.

The moral of the story is that a little bit of real money means a lot more to most people than a lot of play money. A part of the psychology of students who take out student loans is that the money is theoretical, much like play money; but once you start paying it back, it becomes real money out of your budget. At that point, you don't just think about it, you feel it. This is a critical first step in your journey to pay off your loan. Remember, experience is the best training.

Remember Michelle, our medical school student we met many pages ago? What difference would a $1.00 a day make to her, when she is carrying a quarter-million worth of student loans. Truth be told, Michelle's beliefs about money are responsible for her situation. She believed that borrowing was the way to finance her education. Because I don't know all intimate details of her life, I cannot say whether other opportunities were available. Nevertheless, let us see what, if any, difference a dollar-a-day would have made.

In my book, *Easy Money Management,* I

outline a strategy for Giving and Saving a dollar a day. Had she began doing that when she began college, by the time she finished medical school (seven years in all) she would have saved $2,555 (7 @ $365), assuming no gains. She would have given the same amount to someone or some cause that she cared about. In her case because of the student loan, she would have to have paid an additional $1.00 a day against her student loan. By my reckoning, she would have paid $2,555 and still owed ($240,000 - $2,555) $237,445.

What difference does a dollar make when you owe that kind of money? The difference is that in addition to those few dollars a day, she gave, saved, and paid, she gained the powerful intangible asset of experience. To begin, if she had put the dollar saved into an investment account—there are accounts that let you start investing with as little as $100—she would also have gained seven years of real time investing experience. The dollars she gave away, would have gone to someone or some cause that she cared about allowing her to be a blessing to them. An additional bonus of the giving would have been she has had seven years of giving to fill her heart with the gratitude that comes with cheerful giving. Last, she would have built a habit of paying back the money she borrowed. Once the foundational money habits were in place, she could have increased the amounts at any point in her seven-year journey.

In the last chapter I talked about the importance of training. If two people asked you to loan them money, which person would you think was the better credit risk? The person with a seven year track record of giving to others, saving for themselves, and paying what they owe, or the person with none of those skills who after seven years, has no money saved, no history of helping others, and has not paid a single cent on their student loan? For me, it would be the former, but you must decide which works for you.

Action Steps

- Download the <u>FIVE-MINUTE CRASH COURSE</u>, at https://giveandsave365.com and then sign it, date it, and put in somewhere you will see it several times a day.

giveandsave365.com

Teaching you how to use every dollar you get to add value to your life and the lives of others.

GIVE AND SAVE 365 — THE EASY MONEY MANAGEMENT FIVE-MINUTE CRASH COURSE

1. GOING BROKE HABIT OF MONEY MANAGEMENT

YOU MAKE, GET AN ALLOWANCE, OR GIFT OF	$100
YOU SPEND ON BILLS OR PURCHASES	-$100
YOU HAVE LEFT UNTIL YOU GET MORE	$0

2. GOING INTO DEBT HABIT OF MONEY MANAGEMENT

YOU MAKE, GET AN ALLOWANCE, OR GIFT OF	$100
YOU SPENT ON BILLS OR PURCHASES	-$100
YOU BORROWED	-$10
THE NEXT $100 YOU GET YOU ALREADY OWE	-$10

3. GETTING AND STAYING AHEAD HABIT OF MONEY MANAGEMENT

YOU MAKE, GET AN ALLOWANCE, OR GIFT OF	$100
YOU SPENT ON BILLS OR PURCHASES	-$80
YOU SAVED (YOU PAID YOURSELF FIRST)	$10
YOU GAVE (YOU HELPED SOMEBODY)	$10
YOU HAVE LEFT UNTIL YOU GET MORE	+$10

NAME: _____ DATE: _____

We guarantee you will feel good about what you are doing with your money and what your money is doing for you and others.

Thoughts BecomeThings

Henry Ford was once said, "Whether you think you can, or you think you can't you are right." If you think you can't ever pay off your student loan, you are right, you can't. If you think you can pay off your student loan, you can. Your beliefs attract thoughts, things, and people to you. If you made it to college, you had to first think it was possible that you could graduate high school. Beyond that you had to believe, you could get accepted to a college. Once accepted you either thought you could graduate or thought you couldn't. Either you did or you did not and either way you were right.

As I spoke to people across the country about their student loans, there were people who thought their loans were the only way they could afford college and that became their reality. Borrowing for college then became the only way they could afford college. I interviewed a man, Mark, in Arizona. He, his wife, and all three of their children had college degrees and never borrowed a dime. The wife's parents paid for her college, he went on an athletic scholarship, his daughters went on athletic scholarships, and they paid for the son. He thought they did not need student loans to go to college and he was right.

I also interviewed the head of financial aid for a

major college. He, his mother, and father all took out student loans to go to college. He thought that was the only way they could afford it. He was right.

There was a third family, a mother father and two sons and a daughter. One daughter and one son went to state universities and took out loans, while the other son went to a private university on full scholarships. All three had high GPA's and successfully completed advanced courses in high school before applying to college. Same home, same parents, but different thoughts led to different outcomes.

What you think you can do radically affects the people and things you attract. In my earlier chapter, "Who you Wit?" I explained the importance of the people you know and hang with as they influence what you do and how you do it. As part of the research for this book, one question I asked people with student loans was, "Do you know anyone who went to college without taking out a loan.?" Many of them said, "No." The obvious follow-up is, "Is that because everyone in college has student loan debt or is that because everyone '*you know*' that went to college has student loan debt?" When making decisions, many times what you believe to be real is more important than reality. If you limit your world to only people who think and act the way you do, you will believe that is all the world has to offer. Believing you can do better than you have been doing is the beginning of change and

90

growth. How you think, and act affects where you go and whether you grow.

Action Steps

- Write ten ways a person could pay for college without taking out a student loan, whether you believe it is possible or no.

Three Card Monte Find the Lady

Three-Card Monte—also known as Find the Lady and Three-Card Trick–is a confidence game in which the victim, or "mark", is tricked into betting a sum of money, on the assumption that they can find the "money card" among three face-down playing cards. It is very similar to the shell game except that cards are used instead of shells.

In its full form, Three-Card Monte is an example of a classic "short con" in which a shill pretends to conspire with the mark to cheat the dealer, while in fact conspiring with the dealer to cheat the mark.

The mark has no chance whatsoever of winning, at any point in the game. In fact, anyone who is observed winning anything in the game can be presumed to be a shill. When I was conducting my interviews for this book, I asked the interviewees: "Who issued the loan and who will you actually make your payments to?" The answers made me feel like I was playing Three Card Monte, because more than half those interviewed had no idea who issued their loan.

To answer this question, I offer the following article by Sean Ross, published on Investopedia (updated July 30, 2019).

Who Actually Owns Student Loan Debt?

As of Q1 2019, American students were on the hook for approximately $1.49 trillion in student loans. The average borrower owed between $25,000 and $35,000, up significantly from past decades. With that much money on the line, it's reasonable to be curious about who might ultimately receive all those principal and interest payments. While $1.49 trillion may be a significant liability for the borrowers, it can be an even bigger asset for creditors.

The Maze of Student Loan Processing

It is possible for your student loan to have been originated by one institution, be owned by another, guaranteed by yet another and possibly serviced by a fourth or even fifth agency. This can make it very difficult to track down who owns your debt and how. Much also depends on the type of loan you took out, although it is safe to say the federal government was involved in some way.

Most lenders are huge institutions, such as international banks or the government. After a loan is originated, however, it represents an asset that can be bought and sold on the market. Banks are often incentivized to move loans off the books and sell them to another intermediary because doing so instantly improves their capital ratio and allows them to make even more loans. Since almost all loans are fully guaranteed by the government, banks can sell them for a higher price, because default risk is not transferred with the asset.

Non-Government Owners

Outside the government, most student loans are held by the lender or a third-party loan servicing company. Originators and third parties can each perform in-house collection services or contract that duty out to a collection agency. Some of the largest private student loan companies include Navient Corp., Wells Fargo & Co., and Discover Financial Services.

Many student loans are also owned by quasi-governmental agencies or private companies with beneficial relationships with the Department of Education, such as NelNet Inc. and Sallie Mae. Sallie Mae holds a lot of the loans made under the Federal Family Education Loan Program (FFELP),

97

which was replaced by the federal government.

The Federal Government as Creditor

As of July 8, 2016, the federal government owned approximately $1 trillion in outstanding consumer debt, per data compiled by the Federal Reserve Bank of St. Louis. That figure was up from less than $150 billion in January 2009, representing a nearly 600% increase over that time span. The main culprit is student loans, which the federal government effectively monopolized in a little-known provision of the Affordable Care Act, signed into law in 2010.

Prior to the Affordable Care Act, a majority of student loans originated with a private lender but were guaranteed by the government, meaning taxpayers foot the bill if student borrowers default. In 2010, the Congressional Budget Office (CBO) estimated 55% of loans fell into this category.

Between 2011 and 2016, the share of privately originated student loans fell by nearly 90%.

Prior to the administration of Bill Clinton, the federal government owned zero student loans, although it had been in the business of guaranteeing loans since at least 1965. Between the first year of the Clinton presidency and the last year of George W. Bush's administration, the government slowly accumulated about $140 billion in student debt. Those figures have exploded since 2009. In September 2018, the U.S. Treasury Department revealed in its annual report that student loans account for 36.8% of all U.S. government assets.

The cost of federal student loan programs is widely debated. The CBO provides two different estimates based on low discount rates and "fair value" discount rates. If you rely on the fair value estimate, the government loses approximately $100 billion to $250 billion per year, including $40+ billion in administrative costs. In other words, the government does not recoup the value of the loans, putting present and future taxpayers in the position of guarantor. (Article ends here.)

Action Steps

- Identify who owns your student loan(s).

The College Completion Conundrum

One factor that greatly affects the huge amount of student loan being owed is the college completion crisis. The fact that many students take these loans to get a higher education degree because of the need to acquire a post-secondary degree has already been established. However, for many people, life interferes and for various reasons, they are unable to complete their educations. When they fail to complete their degrees, they are less employable and less likely to earn income sufficient to offset the debt they still owe.

If this happens with more and more people, the results are not difficult to imagine. There will be more people unable to pay off their loans and the cycle will continue. If people who were taking out student loans were earning their desired degrees, securing stable jobs that pay well and give the right monetary value for those degrees, chances are that outstanding student loan debt balances would not be where they are today. And where they are is staggering.

In 2015 the U.S. Department of Education published that the default rate amongst those who did not complete their degree is three times as high as the rate of those who completed their degree.

103

This strongly suggests that a major factor responsible for the huge amount of student loan debt is not getting the degree for which the loan was taken.

Action Steps

- Find a mentor that did not finish college and still paid off their student loan.

The Scientific Method

When my son Josh was in elementary school, like countless other elementary students, one of his science assignments was to conduct an experiment using the scientific method. The steps in the scientific method are:

- Ask a question

- Conduct background research

- Propose a hypothesis

- Design and perform an experiment to test your hypothesis

- Record observations and analyze the

meaning of the data

- Draw a conclusion

Josh's experiment was to determine whether ants are attracted to sugar substitutes. It went something like this:

- The hypothesis: Since ants are attracted to sugar and sugar substitutes are sweet ants will be attracted to sugar substitutes.

- Design and perform an experiment to test the hypothesis: We emptied packets of sugar and three different types of substitutes a few inches apart.

- Record observations and analyze the meaning of the data. We repeated our experiment three times moving the sugar to different spots.

- Our conclusion: Sugar ants were not attracted to sugar substitutes.

Okay what the heck do ants, sugar, and science have to do with student loans? The relevance is because the scientific method is equally effective in business and life. Let's view the student loan through the prism of the scientific method.

- The question: Should I borrow money to pay for my college education or to help someone else pay for their college education?

- The background and research: Theoretically, the research has shown that with a college education the borrower will over time make more money than if he or she had not gone to college.

- The hypothesis: With the additional money the borrower can earn because of the degree, he or she will be able to pay back the loan and have more money left over than if he or she had not gotten the degree.

- Design an experiment to test the hypothesis: Here is one of the key challenges to this experiment. To begin with, you must overcome the fallacy of composition. The fallacy here is that because some college graduates secured lucrative careers and were able to payback their loans that this will be true for many borrowers. That may or may not be true. In many cases, many of the people I interviewed found that the job they were able to get did not pay enough for them to live comfortably and pay back their loans.

- Record and analyze observations: In one case the student loan payment ($1,645 per month) precluded a man in his fifties with a master's degree from qualifying to buy a house. In another case, a woman in public office owed more than $100,000. She's in her forties and despite the thousands of people she serves and helps to improve their quality of life, on her current trajectory she will most likely die in debt.

- Conclusion: A degree may or may not help the borrower land a job that pays him or her more than if he or she had not gone to college. Depending on the amount of debt, the borrower could end up with less rather than more disposable income. *(Note: Be courteous and explain why you are asking.)*

Action Steps

- Find three people who are working in a career you are interested in and ask them how much they are making. If you were making what they were, how much money would you have left if your student loan payment was $100, $500, $1,000 per month?

Which Side of the Desk...

When conducting business, it is imperative that you recognize what side of the desk you are sitting on. Are you on the side of the buyer or the seller; the lender or the borrower; the teacher or the student; the counselor or the counseled? This is critical because the advice that works in the best interest of one, may not work in the best interest of the other. The seller wants to sell for the highest possible price, whereas the buyer wants to buy at the lowest possible price. Someone advising the seller will probably offer different tips than someone advising the buyer.

Before I go further, I need to detour here for a second. Many students and teachers I speak with perceive the world of education as a lofty pursuit above the profit-focused world of business. Don't believe it. Not only is education a business, it is a thriving business and here is proof. Abigail Hess, reporting for CNBC wrote:

1971 - 1972 academic year: Private college tuition, fees, room and board: $18,140; Public college in-state tuition, fees, room and board: $8,730.

2017 - 2018 academic year: Private college tuition, fees, room and board: $48,380; Public college in-state tuition, fees, room and board:

$21,400.

Lofty or not, somebody on one side of the desk is getting paid a lot and someone on the other side is paying a lot. That looks, swims, and quacks a lot like a business to me.

Back to the desk

If you go into a car dealership to purchase an automobile, you are on the buyer's side of the desk, while the salesperson is on the dealer's side of the desk. The last salesperson I refused to buy a car from, explained to me how he was fighting with his manager to get me the best deal possible, for the car my son was buying. In a word—bull***t! His job was to craft the deal that made the most money for him and the dealership. This did not upset me, because I understand that a laborer is worthy of his hire. The dishonesty is what ticked me off. Telling me he had been fighting with the finance department for days on the deal, when he did not even have my son's social security number to run his credit. That was one of many inconsistencies I noticed before I kicked him to the curb. In this situation my son who is a college graduate was on one side of the desk, and the salesperson (representing the dealership) was on the other. However, I have bought or leased more than 50 cars in my life, so I understand the process. For that reason, I was able to help my son pivot from an offer with a gouging interest rate and a 72-month loan for a used car, to a manageable lease payment on a brand-new car. It matters who's advising whom on both sides of the desk.

When it comes to student loans, the borrowers I have spoken to were advised by school counselors, family friends, financial aid advisors (who by the way are paid by the institutions they work for), and other students—yikes!—when taking out loans. In his book *Debt Free U*, Zac Bissonnette has a chapter titled "The Four People You Meet on Your Way to College and the Lies They Tell." The four he lists are (1) high school guidance counselors; (2) admissions officers; (3) financial aid officers; (4) family and friends. This is Bissonnette's take on it, but I would add number (5) other students as a fifth entry on the list because many students give

117

what their peers tell them more weight than what others tell them. Also, I am not calling anyone a "liar" because that's a bit acerbic for my taste. I do, however, believe that some people are ill-equipped for the task of advising student loan borrowers. Conversely, the lender's advisors consist or lawyers, accountants, lobbyists, marketers, and more. If you don't believe me, read the MPN, master promissory note for a student loan. An extraordinary brain trust crafted that document to offer the lenders the maximum amount of protection. I am not characterizing this as deceptive or unfair, but as shrewd business practices. In response, the borrowers must become shrewd when entering these relationships. A big part of the shrewdness depends on who the borrowers have on their side of the desks.

One last warning here, be careful of persons dispensing secondhand advice that the giver of the advice has not tested and verified on their own. One man I interviewed said he was not worried about the loans, because he knew the government would eventually forgive them. What is more dangerous than his belief in this unproven assertion, is that he advised he daughter to take out loans based on that premise. To draw a line from the movie Scarface, "I always tell the truth, even when I lie." Of course, this man's daughter would believe her father knows what he is talking about even if he doesn't.

Action Steps

- Get one person on your side of the desk who has successfully borrowed and paid off their student loan(s).

I + V = R
(Imagination + Vividness = Reality)

Imagine it's your college graduation day. Your friends and family are in the audience. You're so happy you are almost levitating above your seat. This was not high school, where someone woke you every day and made sure you did your homework, this was college, where you woke yourself up and decided to complete your assignments. Every day was not pretty, and all classes weren't fun, but you did it.

Or you decided later in life, you wanted more

and went back to school as an adult. With all the grownup responsibilities—maybe a spouse, a child, an elderly parent—you still got your butt back in school and now it is graduation day. You finished.

Now, imagine you are debt free. Even if you're not, you can imagine you are and remember Einstein said, "Imagination is more important than fact." And Imagination + Vividness = Reality. And what you believe reality to be is what you act on.

I believe you can have your cake and eat it too. You can have a college education and no debt. You can own your future. I believe the best time to have a Student Loan Exit Plan was the day you took the loan, but the second-best time is now. Right here, right now, turn and head toward the

Exit. My team and I will be waiting for your there.

You got this!

Action Steps

- Henry Ford said, "Obstacles are those frightful things you see when you take your eyes off your goals." See, hear, smell, taste, and feel what it is like to own your future. You got this!

THE END

Acknowledgements

Kim, my wife and the mother of my children. Mom was right, you were the right one for me.

My sons Joshua and Jawanza; you're two of my heroes and you inspire me to never stop learning nor trying new things.

My mother Arimentha Ingram, who even on welfare, with eleven children, scraped together enough money to buy me books that taught me the magic of reading.

Harold "Sonny" Ingraham, my brother from another mother, who taught me if you make a dollar, save a dime.

My brother Ronald, for demonstrating what faith in action looks like.

Arena "Toy" Ingram, my sister who always believed in me even when I did not believe in myself.

My best friend, NBA Scout Irving Thomas, who taught me that talent without work is like a shiny new sports car with no fuel; it may look flashy, but it is not going anywhere.

Bonnie Glover, Esq., author, entrepreneur, NAACP Image award winner, mother, and kidney transplant recipient, for her invaluable insights.

Craig Glover (Bonnie's hubby), MBA, kidney donor, good friend, mentor in the area of entrepreneurship and community building.

Matthew Glover (Bonnie's eldest), Yale alumnus, City University of New York (CUNY) School of Law graduate, for superb critique of this manuscript.

Bishop Victor T. Curry, M. Div., PhD, and my New Birth Baptist Church Cathedral of Faith International (COFI) family for all the prayers and support. The best is not yet to come, the best is here.

Doug Saenz, Terence Bentley, Mike O'Donnell and Cohort 7 of Broward College, Career Source Broward / StartUp Now; for helping me get the Student Loan Exit Plan from my imagination to reality.

Florida International University Vice-President El Pagnier K. Hudson for her support and introductions.

Kishasha B. Sharp, Esq., my sister-in-law, for her continued encouragement and suggestions.

Roderick Harvey, CPA, CVA, for demonstrating excellence in service and supporting me in my ventures over the years.

Armstrong Creative Consulting: Da-Venya, you and Sam are to Give and Save 365, what icing is to a birthday cake.

About the Author

Laurick Ingram, Director of Give and Save 3-6-5, created The Student Loan Exit Plan, to engage and educate borrowers on how to pay off these debts as quickly as possible and put money back in their accounts. He graduated from Miami Central High School (Go Rockets!) and has a degree in Business Administration from Miami Dade College. In 2018, the United Nations Association (Broward Chapter) honored him for his efforts to eradicate poverty. In 2019 Legacy Miami, Legacy South Florida and MIA Magazines named him one of Florida's Most Powerful Black Business Leaders. He has been interviewed on radio and television and has been mentioned in hundreds of journals and publications.

www.ingramcontent.com/pod-product-compliance
Lightning Source LLC
Chambersburg PA
CBHW062010200326
41519CB00017B/4741